BRITAIN IN OLD PI

IPSWICH
REVISITED

DAVID KINDRED

SUTTON PUBLISHING LIMITED

Sutton Publishing Limited
Phoenix Mill · Thrupp · Stroud
Gloucestershire · GL5 2BU

First published 1996

Cover photographs: (front) the flags were
flying on Bishops Hill in June 1930 for a
visit by the Prince of Wales (*see* page 33);
(back) a charming Christmas picture from
the 1930s (*see* pages 66–7).

British Library Cataloguing in Publication Data
A catalogue record for this book is available from the
British Library.

ISBN 0-7509-1325-8

Typeset in 10/12 Perpetua.
Typesetting and origination by
Sutton Publishing Limited.
Printed in Great Britain by
Ebenezer Baylis, Worcester.

CONTENTS

A girl in the garden of her home in Ipswich, *c.* 1920. The photograph captures the fashion for clothes and toys perfectly. Her coat and hat are a copy of adults' of the period, as are her doll's pram and clothes.

INTRODUCTION

Welcome to *Ipswich Revisited*, a fascinating look at Ipswich from years ago. For many, memories will come flooding back as they look at the town and events of yesteryear, with pictures not only of the town and its streets, but also of its people; the way they worked, lived and played.

Ipswich is a town where folk have deep roots. Generations of the same families have always lived locally. You can find a common acquaintance in a room of half a dozen strangers at any gathering in town; it's just one big village, and everybody knows somebody their friends and relatives know. This gives a sense of belonging, and leads to a great interest in local history, unlike many other towns, packed with commuters who do not even know their neighbours.

Photography has provided a marvellous medium to record detail; everybody finds some different point of interest in any photograph. A simple street scene will catch the eye of some who are interested in vintage transport, while others will be reminded of their favourite shops or public house, while many find the clothes of passers-by fascinating.

As soon as photography was invented in the late 1830s it naturally became the perfect means to record life. There is a Hollywood myth of the past, perfectly tailored clothes, pristine cars and machines, and well-fed faces. But the study of old photographs soon dispels this image: life was very often harsh, and no amount of re-creation captures the mood. Sadly, much is not recorded on film. Old, often shabby, housing is swept away without being photographed, and all that remains are a few memories, soon lost forever as the generations pass. There is much of the town from the past that I have never seen – the housing around Rope Walk and The Mount, for example. Unless commissioned, professional photographers do not generally record street scenes, and even though most people now have access to a camera, how many of them take pictures of a town's streets today? What was often rather mundane when old pictures were taken becomes the point of interest years later. A row of shops is not the greatest challenge to a photographer, and parked cars were usually in the way at the time, but now the vehicles and shops are of intense interest with the passing of the years. Often in Edwardian postcard scenes there is a group of children in the foreground. Perhaps the photographer would have preferred them out of the way, but now, some ninety years later, those children bring the picture to life.

The end of the Second World War in 1945 was cause for great celebration. Although the war continued in the Far East, VE-Day saw many street parties in Ipswich. I have featured several pictures from that period of joy. Many pictures would have been taken on simple box cameras, but they are no less important than the pictures taken by Reg Fisk of Tudor Photos, who toured the town and took many pictures of the street parties.

I have devoted a large number of pictures to the 1950s, a time of great change in the town; many who were around then will enjoy the memories of those years. Some wonderful images capture the decade perfectly.

Thousands will recall the heyday of speedway racing at Foxhall Stadium, when the 'Witches' were formed in the early fifties. People flocked to the track at the edge of town when exciting live entertainment was much needed after the difficult times of the war years. Many locals can still recall

names such as Sid Clarke, 'Titch' Read and Bert Edwards from the speedway era. I have included se
pictures from the camera of Don Harris at Foxhall Stadium; he was a regular in the pits and on the t.
bend with his quarter-plate camera.

I am often asked where all the photographs in my collection have come from. There is a simple
answer. Often, old collections of unidentified, unprinted negatives turn up. I am always interested in
exploring these, and as a professional photographer I have the knowledge and the facilities to bring out
the best in the pictures. I did not set out to become a collector of photographs, but simply decided,
around eight years ago, to collect a few examples of Victorian techniques, having seen a daguerreotype
belonging to a friend and photographic colleague, Terry Neeves. One glass negative led to a few more,
and now I have many images that I am convinced would have been otherwise thrown away for want of a
home. I am able to share them through the pages of the *Evening Star*, of which I am the picture editor, and
this series of books. This is the fourth book of photographs from my collection. Each time, I have thought
'this is the last book', but often a phone call will lead to someone who has more negatives in need of care.

The postcard photographers who sold pictures of events, disasters and local street scenes provided a
rich vein of pictures. No photographers work in this way now, selling pictures, often door to door, of
small events and street scenes, so this type of record simply does not exist now. I have copied picture
postcards in ones and twos and over the years they have built up into a comprehensive set of once
scattered images. I have made every effort to date the photographs accurately, and I trust that the
information on the back of the prints is largely correct. You reach the point where you can check no
more, so forgive me if you know better! I hope you enjoy this book.

David Kindred, 1996

A party in Beck Street to celebrate the Coronation of Queen Elizabeth II in June 1953.

AROUND THE TOWN

Staff and customers of Walter Carter's bakery at the corner of Brooks Hall Road and Norwich Road pose for the camera, c. 1900.

Bramford Road at the junction of Prospect Road (right), *c.* 1912.

Another view of Bramford Road, this one at the corner of Bulwer Road, *c.* 1912. This photo features a charming group of children watching the photographer at work. The shop on the corner is W. and E. Denny's pork butchers shop offering 'Dairy fed pork' and 'Home made Sausages'.

Ransomes, Sims & Jefferies is an Ipswich company world famous for its grass-cutting equipment. One of their local customers in the 1890s was the gardener at Rushmere Villa. This print from an original glass negative is titled simply 'Albert and mowing machine'.

Robinson's newsagents at the corner of Back Hamlet and Grove Lane, *c.* 1915. The business moved to 137 Foxhall Road in about 1930.

The main buildings shown here in Bridge Street, including the Crown public house (centre) have all been demolished and the site is now part of the Stoke Bridge traffic system. The same view today would feature the Novotel hotel.

An enterprising service in the 1930s was this mobile Home Services Library from Copdock, offering a selection of humour, romance, and mystery titles.

A delivery boy from Brewer's grocery stores, St Matthews Street, pauses for the camera of keen photographer Percy Chinery, near his home in London Road. Mr Chinery also took the top picture. The allotments shown in the background of both pictures are still there today.

This postcard view from around 1910 is titled 'Majors Corner'. It features Bond Street, the Mitre Tavern (left) on the corner of St Helens Street, and Majors Corner in the middle distance. The man on the ladder is working on the County Hall building.

Another postcard view, this one shows St Helens Street looking towards Majors Corner, with the County Hall in the centre, *c.* 1918. On the extreme right is the Great Eastern Railways receiving office with Lancelot Ashford's piano tuning business beyond at no. 53.

A postcard view of St Helens Street and the corner of Regent Street (left), *c.* 1907. The spire of St Helens Church is visible at top right.

The Belvedere public house in Cox Lane in the late 1920s. This part of the town housed a thriving community in its tiny streets, now all cleared to make way for a car park. The pub was rebuilt as the General Gordon and is now the Earl Roberts.

The wedding of Florence Clarke and Frank Townsend at St Bartholomew's Church, 17 February 1928. This charming group captures the fashions of the era perfectly.

Staff from the self-raising department at Cranfield Brothers Ltd, flour millers, of St Peters Street, in the 1920s.

A rather serious group of girls at St Margarets School in 1928. Most of the girls are wearing smock tops to keep their clothes clean. It was still the norm for photographers taking group pictures to include a slate with the group's identity chalked on it; this one simply says 'St Margarets Group II'.

Ranelagh Road from near the junction with Ancaster Road (right), *c.* 1915. Almost all the houses on the left have been demolished.

Fore Street, *c.* 1910. At this time, the street was full of shops serving the local community, most of whom lived in terraced housing in the dock area. On the left at nos 90–92 is C.B. Gyford's fruiterers and greengrocers. The lady is looking in the window of Edward Haggar's butchers shop, next door to the Old Neptune inn.

F.W. Woolworth's store in Carr Street in the 1920s. All of the buildings on the right, including the Lyceum Theatre and the offices and printing works of the *East Anglian Daily Times* and *Evening Star* have since been replaced by the Eastgate shopping centre.

This is the reverse view to the picture above and shows Carr Street with the Lyceum Theatre in the foreground. The theatre was built in 1890–1 at a cost of £9,000, but closed in 1936.

An Edwardian view showing the junction of Felixstowe Road and Bishops Hill. On the left is a drinking trough for horses.

Felixstowe Road, with Alston Road leading off to the right, *c.* 1910.

Herbert Wells' butchers shop in Fore Street (opposite the swimming baths) attracted huge queues in the 1940s for his sausages. Also shown are F.J. Southgate, hairdresser, and Smyth Brothers, ironmongers.

Lord Haldane inspecting some immaculately turned out nurses during his visit to the town on 13 May 1911.

Here the guard of honour stands to attention as Lord Haldane steps into his car after opening the new drill hall in Great Gipping Street.

Lord Kitchener also visited Ipswich, where he attended a scout rally at Portman Road sports ground (where the football club is today). Here Kitchener, wearing a blue serge suit and bowler hat, is inspecting the scouts. Reports said 'photographers were firing at his Lordship without intermission, but he seemed unconcerned'.

The scouts enjoyed an open air tea party after Lord Kitchener's visit.

Cliff Quay now stands where children played in the 1920s. On the right is the huge gasometer at the gas works near the wet dock. Work to enlarge the port began in 1923, extending along land known as Hogg Highland, a popular tree-lined area. Steam-powered piling equipment can be seen in the centre.

A postcard view from the gasometer, overlooking the lock gates, 1920s. In the centre and now replaced by the West Bank terminal, is Stoke bathing place, an open air swimming pool that was little more than a walled off area of the River Orwell with changing huts.

Lloyds Avenue from Tower Ramparts, early 1930s. The arch through the Lloyds building on the Cornhill was cut during 1929 and opened to traffic on 5 January 1930.

A postcard view of Tavern Street, looking towards the junction of Dial Lane and Tower Street, *c.* 1915.

Staff pose outside George Bernard's coffee house at 42 St Margarets Street. Next door is the premises of John Spencer, chimney cleaner.

Northgate School photographed from the air soon after it opened in the 1930s.

Bixley Road, part of the new by-pass, in the 1930s. This view from near the junction with Felixstowe Road shows an almost traffic-free road.

A huge fire completely destroyed the premises of R.D. & J.B. Fraser in April 1912. Built in 1890 at the corner of Museum Street and Princes Street, the store was rebuilt after the fire and today houses an insurance office.

Another huge blaze in Ipswich wrecked E.R. & F. Turner Limited's engineering works in Quadling Street early this century. Postcard photographers were quick to feed the public's fascination with disaster at a time when local newspapers did not yet include photographs with their reports.

Church bell-founder Alfred Bowell had premises in Wykes Bishop Street, which used to run from Fore Hamlet to near the dock. This picture shows members of his staff with bells for Ditchingham Church, Norfolk, in 1931.

Staff at Alfred Bowell's pose with bells for Kirby-le-Soken Church, Essex.

Argyle Street from St Helens Street, *c.* 1908. The school building on the left is now part of University College, Suffolk. Many of the houses on the right were demolished in the 1950s (*see* page 106).

Burlington Road from Barrack Corner, *c.* 1905.

Crowds filled the Cornhill in September 1905 to see General William Booth, the founder of the Salvation Army.

The proclamation of King George V, who succeeded to the throne in 1910, was another event that had crowds thronging the Cornhill.

This postcard view from Wherstead Road shows the junction of Vernon Street and Austin Street (left), *c.* 1915. The public house on the left, Uncle Tom's Cabin (now the Orwell Mariner) was a popular ale house for the residents of the hundreds of terraced houses in the area. All of the buildings except the pub have now gone, including the fine house and horse drinking trough on the right. Once again, notice the almost traffic-free streets.

Flags flying on the Duke of Sussex public house in Cumberland Street to celebrate the Coronation of King George VI on 12 May 1937.

A policeman on point duty, directing traffic at the busy junction of Tavern Street and Carr Street, c. 1905. The White Horse Hotel's frontage has been altered in recent years and now includes shops.

The Prince of Wales, later (briefly) King Edward VIII, flew in from Northolt to perform the official opening of Ipswich's airport. Later that day he visited Ransomes, Sims & Jefferies' Orwell Works in Duke Street. This photograph was taken as he travelled down Bishops Hill, near the junction with Myrtle Road, where the 'Long Live the Prince' sign is. Almost everything in this picture has been demolished. The houses in the foreground are also featured on page 52.

The world famous Barnum and Bailey circus came to Ipswich in 1898 and 1899, attracting huge crowds to the town. Based at a site near Bramford Road, the circus animals were paraded through the town. These four photographs were taken as they came down Fonnereau Road.

Here, teams of zebra pull floats featuring nursery rhyme characters.

The huge team of circus horses about to turn on to St Margarets Plain.

Armoured knights paraded on horseback in 1898. The buildings on the right have now been replaced by the Bethesda Baptist Church.

The Wolsey Pageant was held in Christchurch Park during the 1930s. These ladies pose on the steps of a special set built in front of Christchurch Mansion.

Spring Road with Bartholomew Street off to the right, *c.* 1912.

These buildings at the corner of St Margarets Street (right) and Soane Street were altered during the widening of St Margarets Street in the early 1930s. The right half was rebuilt with the gable ends 'turned' to face St Margarets Street (*see* below).

St Margarets Plain, 1950. On the right is the building featured in the top picture. The Running Buck public house is on the left.

A Christmas card showing the Ancient House bookshop, 1908.

This new building in Tacket Street was photographed in the mid-1930s. G.W. Hales, dispensing chemist, and photographic specialist, was then the main occupier of the building.

The passengers of a horse and buggy pose outside the premises of Charles Ingham, Beer Retailer, at nos 76 and 78 Woodbridge Road, near Argyle Street.

W. Webster, photographer of The Studio Royal, 105 St Helens Street, took this picture outside his premises (right) in the mid-1890s. The site is now part of Wells Court flats.

Fore Hamlet from the bottom of Bishops Hill, late 1940s. The van is just passing the entrance to Cavendish Street, off to the right.

An Edwardian view of Finchley Road. In those days it was lit with gas lamps.

Ipswich. Meet of the Hounds in Constable Road, 1902.

A meet of the hounds in Constable Road, 1902.

The Old Manor House on St Margarets Green still stands today although the ivy and the iron railings shown here have disappeared.

In medieval times the Cornhill, or Market Hill as it was also known, was the town's principal trading centre. The earliest known plan of Ipswich, drawn in 1610, shows how the main roads through the town converged at this point. Throughout the history of the borough it has been a meeting place for large gatherings and markets. The post office building on the right replaced the Corn Exchange in 1881. This picture was taken in the 1920s looking towards Tavern Street from the window of Grimwades shop. Two single-decker trolley buses, which came into service in the mid-1920s to replace the trams, are featured in the foreground.

A postcard view of the Town Hall (right) and post office, *c.* 1912. The line of taxis is an interesting mixture of motor cars and horse-drawn cabs. The cab ranks moved to Lloyds Avenue when it opened in 1930.

The Cornhill, looking into Westgate Street in the early 1930s. This is the reverse view of the Cornhill from the picture shown opposite. The Lloyds Avenue arch, which opened in 1930, and Footman's Waterloo House store (now Debenhams) are on the right.

Derby Road railway station, *c.* 1890. The line from Ipswich to Felixstowe opened in May 1877.

Tacket Street Congregational Church, 1930. The demolition of shops on the corner of Cox Lane gave a much better view of the church. The twin spires have since been removed and the church renamed Christchurch. The pawnbrokers' sign (top right) belonged to Bradbrook's clothiers shop at 1 Orwell Place; they also offered a pawnbroking service.

A cargo of sugar being unloaded at Flint Wharf in the wet dock, 1920s. The sugar was for Burton, Son & Sanders Ltd, wholesale grocers and provision merchants, of College Street.

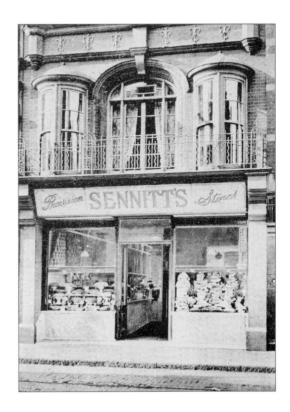

A 1920s promotional card for Frederick Sennitt's provision store at 18 Carr Street.

A huge blaze destroyed parts of R. & W. Paul's site at Ipswich dock on 24 January 1910. This picture 'taken at midnight' by Tunn and Company was one of a series of postcards of the disaster on sale to the public.

This fine pair of horse and carts belonged to Walter Pipe and Company of Derby Road, who offered the 'Finest House Coals'. The numbers on the front of the horses would seem to suggest that they were taking part in a competition.

TRANSPORT

This section of the book looks at various forms of transport, many of which influenced the town's development. Ipswich's origins lie in the River Orwell, the port and the crossing point at Stoke Bridge, while the construction of the wet dock, which opened in 1842, brought extra trade to the heart of the town. The railway from London was completed in June 1846, making travel easier for the masses. This splendid sailing ship, the Arthur Fitger, *is pictured in the wet dock on 18 April 1900.*

The Great Eastern Railway Company ran a paddle-steamer service from the New Cut (shown here), Ipswich to Harwich and Felixstowe between 1895 and 1930. The trees in the background were part of a popular promenade lost through commercial development of the island site during the 1920s.

Two young ladies with their cycles at Rushmere in 1900. Their style of dress must have made cycling difficult.

The charabanc, a mixture of open-topped bus and car, was a popular means of transport for days out. Public houses often arranged trips to the coast or visits to country pubs for darts competitions and so on. No doubt loaded with a few beers, this group is leaving the Vernon Arms in Whip Street, sometime in the 1920s.

Another outing from the Vernon Arms. Unlike the charabanc in the top picture, this one did not have the new pneumatic tyres to smooth the ride.

Electric trams came into service in 1903, replacing the horse-drawn vehicle service. They ran on main routes to the edge of town until they were in turn replaced in the 1920s by the trolley bus or 'trackless trams'. The last electric tram service ran in July 1926. The elegant Edwardian couple were waiting to cross at the Wherstead Road terminus.

An electric tram on Bishops Hill, at the junction with Myrtle Road (right), *c.* 1905.

A row of double-decker trolley buses outside the Royal Showground at Chantry in 1934. A special service was arranged to transport the thousands of visitors to the Show from the town centre. The Showground now lies under the Chantry housing estate. All these buses were built by Ransomes, Sims & Jefferies in 1933 and 1934.

A single-decker trolley bus, built by Ransomes, Sims & Jefferies, in Adair Road in 1926. This unit was withdrawn from service in 1950 and used as a store at Pakefield near Lowestoft, and was later acquired by Ipswich Transport Society for preservation.

This trolley bus overturned on Bishops Hill on 8 June 1955.

Another accident – trolley bus 123 collided with the Crown public house in Bridge Street, sometime in the 1950s.

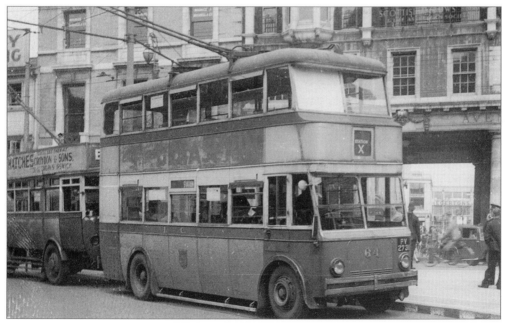

Trolley bus 64, built by Ransomes, Sims & Jefferies in 1936, on the Cornhill. This 48-seater was withdrawn from service in 1951. Originally sold to a dealer of Church Lane, Sproughton, it was bought in 1952 by a fruit merchant who used it as a shed at his premises in Sproughton Road. It was finally broken up on 5 November 1964.

Crown Street, early 1960s. Trolley bus 107 turns from Tower Rampart bus station on to Crown Street, passing Egertons garage. The garage site is now occupied by Crown Pools.

A new ticket machine in use on an Ipswich trolley bus, 30 August 1951. Trolley buses were taken out of service in August 1963.

Horse-drawn taxi cabs lined up outside the post office on the Cornhill, 16 March 1900.

Taxi cabs outside the post office, *c*. 1910.

The great days of steam trains are recalled by these two pictures. At Ipswich station in 1931 is a class B17/2 locomotive, number 2810, *Honningham Hall* of the London & North Eastern Railway Company. The train was the express for Cambridge, and the first coach was a six-wheel Great Eastern clerestory dating from the turn of the century.

A class D15, no. 8880, piloting an unidentified class B17 at the station, also in 1931.

SPORT & LEISURE

In this section we will look at some of the sport and leisure activities that local folk have enjoyed during the past hundred years. The first pictures include some remarkable photographs taken of amateur sports in and around Rushmere at the turn of the century. We also look at early tennis fashion, speedway in its heyday in the 1950s, cricket and football. This photograph shows the ladies' cricket teams from Rushmere and Falkenham in the late 1890s.

This charming sports scene from the 1890s shows the Rushmere ladies' cricket team posed for the camera seated on a farm wagon. Their formal dress (by today's standards) must have made it very difficult for them to run and field. Almost everybody is wearing a hat for the event. The picture helps break down the myth that Victorians were all stern-faced – by this time photography was 'instantaneous', removing the need to sit perfectly still for several seconds which made it so difficult to hold a smile.

Another picture from the Rushmere vs Falkenham ladies' cricket match, with a fine selection of fashions from the period.

Rushmere vs Playford. It is difficult to believe the lady holding the bat could stay long at the wicket dressed as she is; although the bowler probably could not even see the wicket, cries of 'skirt before wicket' would have sounded a little odd!

Gentlemen modelling their tennis outfits at Rushmere in the late 1890s.

A fine pair at the wicket at Rushmere in the 1890s.

Hardly the 'leggy' look of modern tennis for these elegant young ladies at Rushmere in the 1890s.

It is not clear whether this picture was taken as a joke. The rather stern faces suggest not, but exactly why the Ipswich Tramways football team should be wearing top hats for their team photograph in 1906 we might never know. The Tramways service would have had a large staff of both drivers and conductors from which to select their teams. At the Constantine Road depot there was a large maintenance crew, and the town's first power station and waste disposal incinerator was run by the Tramways service. The power station was built to provide a service for the electric trams, although electricity was also supplied to domestic and commercial users. It was replaced by Cliff Quay power station in the 1950s. The town's refuse was also disposed of in an incinerator at the site. The 178½ ft chimney that served the site was demolished in the 1950s but the other buildings are still standing, and part still functions as the main depot and offices for Ipswich Buses Ltd.

A more conventional Ipswich Tramways team.

Gainsborough Athletic football club team, season 1932/33.

The Orwell Works athletic club team of Ransomes, Sims & Jefferies with their trophies, *c.* 1912.

Ipswich Town football club team, season 1906/07.

Many happy hours were spent on the *River Lady* which took pleasure trippers on the River Orwell from New Cut to Harwich Harbour, on the same route taken years earlier by the paddle-steamers of the Great Eastern Railway (*see* page 48). This picture was taken on 24 May 1956 as the vessel neared Bourne Bridge. In the background are the three distinctive chimneys of Cliff Quay power station.

The Ipswich Sports at the Portman Road sports ground in 1912 included a tug-o'-war event.

A family Christmas before the age of television. In those days everybody gathered for the day to enjoy traditional games. The pictures on these two pages were taken by keen amateur photographer 'Charlie' Girling of Powling Road. Mr Girling recorded events in the town spanning seven decades. This picture from the 1930s shows his family and friends gathered for a typical Christmas tea with chicken, celery, pickles, jelly, and mince pies. Paper hats from the Christmas crackers are another feature of the picture. Mr Girling's final picture project was the construction of the Buttermarket shopping centre, which he photographed when he was in his eighties!

A festive game of snooker. Photographer Mr Girling is on the left.

Playing bagatelle. A present for one of the children, the game was evidently enjoyed by all.

Speedway racing came to Ipswich when Foxhall Stadium was built in 1950. Every Thursday night throughout the early and mid-1950s, crowds of up to twenty thousand people would make their way to the stadium to cheer on 'The Witches'. Spectators either walked, cycled, or took special buses to the stadium at this time since relatively few had motor transport of their own to reach the track. Pictured here at a practice session are John Laurie (left), Bob Sharpe (centre), and Dennis Day.

'The Witches' team, 1956. On the bike is team captain Bert Edwards and standing behind him, from left to right, are 'Junior' Bainbridge, Len Silver, Bill Bryden, Bob Sharpe, Ken Last and 'Titch' Read.

A capacity crowd at the stadium in April 1953. Here, from left to right, Johnnie Chamberlain, Harold NcNaughton, and 'Titch' Read break from the start.

'Witches' Bert Edwards (left) and 'Junior' Bainbridge on the concrete start grid.

First bend action from the 1950s with Dennis Day (left) and Sid Clarke in the lead.

Managers and team members handing out the food and drink at the 'Witches' supporters club Christmas party.

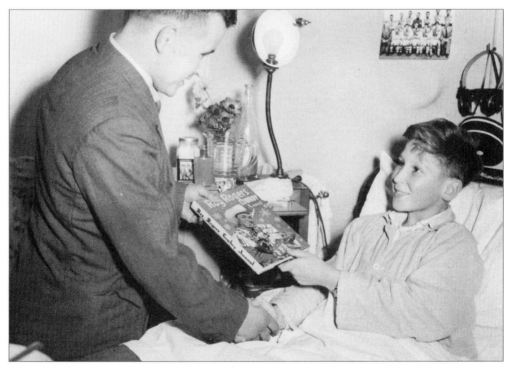

This young patient in hospital at Christmas time 1955 was no doubt cheered up by a visit from speedway rider 'Titch' Read who presented him with a copy of the Roy Rogers Christmas Annual.

'Titch' Read, dressed as a schoolboy, hands out the gifts at the 'Witches' Christmas party in 1955.

The Ipswich speedway team, 1957. Back row, left to right: Otto Holubeck, Bob Sharpe, Cyril Roger, Peter Moore, Danny Dunton. Front row: Len Silver, Bert Edwards, 'Junior' Bainbridge.

The Ipswich team lined up on the centre green in front of another huge crowd, 25 April 1953.

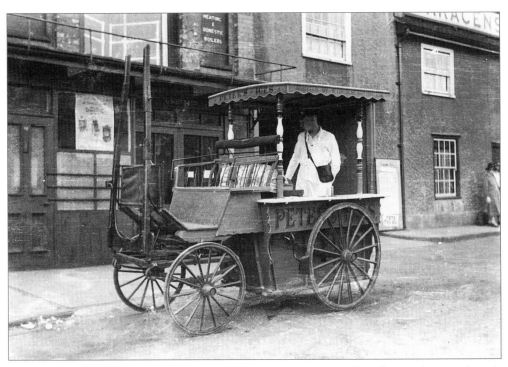

Almost every fête, fun day and sports event featured a Peters ice-cream seller. This popular Ipswich-made ice-cream holds fond memories for generations of Ipswich children. A horse-drawn wagon was one sales point, photographed here on St Margarets Green by Percy Chinery in 1933.

A hand cart of Peters ice-cream in London Road in the 1930s.

VICTORY CELEBRATIONS

*The grim years of the Second World War came to an end in May 1945. Although the war continued in
the Far East it was time to celebrate victory in Europe. Street parties were held all over Ipswich. The next
few pictures show hundreds of smiling faces celebrating the good news. This photograph is another from
the camera of 'Charlie' Girling, who is actually in the picture holding the clacker alarm. It was taken
at Cowell's printing works and shows the air raid wardens who worked through the war years to help
defend the town.*

Lancing Avenue.

Long Street.

Bramford Lane.

Grange Road.

Gatacre Road.

Brunswick Road.

More smiles in Brunswick Road.

Thousands attended the VE-Day celebrations on Tower Ramparts car park (now the bus station). Bands played and children danced. In the background is Tower Ramparts School, now the site of the shopping centre.

Golf Hotel, Foxhall Road.

Sidegate Lane.

Waterworks Street.

Phoenix Road.

Leighton Road.

More celebrations on the Gainsborough estate.

Brookfield Road.

Beech Grove.

THE FIFTIES & SIXTIES

As with so many towns, the fifties and sixties saw huge changes in Ipswich. Old housing in the town centre was cleared to make way for road schemes and commercial development, and the population moved into housing estates like Chantry and Maidenhall. Fortunately the largely Victorian Cornhill buildings survived. In this section we will see some of those changes in progress and also capture some of the flavour of life in the town in this period of change. This picture, taken from the Lloyds building in 1951, shows cars parked in front of the Town Hall and queues for buses on what is now a pedestrianized area.

Lloyds Avenue, 3 April 1956. Footmans store is on the left.

Princes Street covered in a tangle of trolley bus wires. This picture is undated but it was probably taken on the same day as the one above.

The Cornhill from the first-floor window of the Golden Lion Hotel in 1951. A policeman on point duty is controlling traffic at the entrance to Lloyds Avenue, and cars park freely around the town centre.

Another view of the Cornhill in 1951.

The Cornhill, looking towards Westgate Street, *c.* 1960.

A postcard view of the Cornhill from near the Town Hall in the early 1960s.

The horse drinking trough on the corner of Portman Road and Princes Street was dismantled and removed on 17 January 1961.

The Hippodrome Theatre in St Peters Street opened on 28 March 1905 and offered music hall and pantomime shows. Film shows started in 1930. The building closed as a theatre in 1957. It became the Savoy ballroom and a bingo hall before demolition in 1985.

Australian acrobat Eddie Ash performing an amazing stunt on the roof of the Hippodrome in the mid-1950s.

Two photographs of the conversion of the Hippodrome in June 1959. The seats had to be lifted to make way for the dance floor, and the piano was removed from the stage.

The Cobbold family's mansion in Holywells Park was built in 1814. Lord Woodbridge purchased the park and mansion in the 1920s and presented them to the town. In its latter years the mansion served as a community centre and youth club but it fell into disrepair and was demolished in 1962. The stable block and clock tower are still there but there are now gardens on the site of the mansion. This photograph was taken on 13 April 1959.

During the 1950s an otter caused considerable damage to the pond life in Holywells Park. It was eventually caught by hounds. Here the hunters proudly show off their catch in front of the mansion.

A market trader in London Road shows the crowd a fine pair of stockings during the 1950s.

Bananas on sale in the market in the 1950s.

A parade of elephants from Chipperfields circus makes its ponderous way along Ranelagh Road from the station on 27 March 1955. Visiting circuses used a site at the corner of Ranelagh Road and London Road.

Elephants from Chipperfields circus in Princes Street on 3 October 1961.

The car park at Tower Ramparts, 3 August 1956. This is now the Tower Ramparts bus station. The large building on the left was Tower Ramparts School. In the centre is Electric House, the showrooms and offices of Eastern Electricity. Egerton's garage in Crown Street is on the right.

The Beehive Inn at the corner of Upper Orwell Street (left) and Carr Street opened in 1899. This view from near the Regent Theatre (then the Gaumont), was taken on 23 March 1960, shortly before its demolition.

A view along Carr Street, 27 January 1965. The buildings look very similar today, with the former site of the Beehive on the left.

Little Colman Street from Carr Street, with part of the *East Anglian Daily Times* and *Evening Star* offices and printing works, in 1965. Newspapers were published on this site from 1887 until 1966 when the company moved to its present site in Lower Brook Street. The company's fleet of delivery vans is lined up outside. The Eastgate shopping centre now stands on this site although the through way to Great Colman Street remains.

Carr Street from White Horse Corner, 13 February 1964. On the right is Heppells chemist shop with, beyond, Lavey's outfitters, Hawkins & Sons Ltd, cotton goods shop, and Mac Fisheries Ltd.

A dinner held by the Ipswich Gardeners Club in the Coop Hall in Carr Street, *c.* 1950.

The Old Cattle Market, 12 October 1959. This view from Cowells printing works shows the post office sorting office (centre left), and at the top of the picture the Blue Coat Boy public house, the Eastern Counties bus station and the Plough public house.

Tacket Street, 24 August 1958. The shops are Hawes & Sons, clothiers and tailors, Ward's grocery store, and the Tankard public house. All of these buildings have since been demolished.

The same row of buildings photographed from the other end of the street on the same day. The Salvation Army Citadel in the foreground was demolished in 1996.

The Buttermarket from Dial Lane, 17 March 1966. The shops on the left include R. Barrett, jewellers, Croasdale chemist, Murdoch's domestic appliances and music shop, and Cowells store.

The arch by St Matthew's Church neatly frames the demolition work in progress to clear the tiny streets of St Matthews Church Lane, Stirling Street, Castle Street and Perth Street, photographed on 27 April 1959. Civic Drive now takes the route of St Matthews Church Lane and the Civic Centre car park is not far from the site of these tiny streets.

The boiler house chimney of St Matthews Baths being demolished in January 1965. This was a time of great change in this part of the town, with the new road scheme under construction, cutting through to the dock area. The muddy outline of Civic Drive and the huge underground car park, still being built at this time, are visible in the background (top left).

St Matthews Street was greatly changed by redevelopment in the 1960s. This postcard view of the street from the mid-1950s shows the junction with Berners Street (left). In the centre is the old Queen's Head public house which was demolished and replaced with a new version built close to the original site. The St Matthews Street roundabout is in the centre of this view today.

St Matthews Street, 7 November 1962. Most of the buildings on the left, including the seventeenth-century Golden Fleece Hotel, were demolished during the 1960s redevelopment of the area. The studios of BBC Radio Suffolk now stand behind the site of the Golden Fleece.

The Queen's Head Hotel, at the corner of St Matthews Street and St Matthews Church Lane, 1965. This is the view from what is now the roundabout.

St Matthews Street, looking towards Barrack Corner, in 1962. The shops which stood in front of St Matthews Baths had been demolished by this time (*see* page 104).

St Matthews Baths also served as a hall during the winter months, with the swimming pool boarded over. Here members of the Women's Institute are holding their annual general meeting on 15 March 1966.

Demolition work under way in Argyle Street in the late 1950s to clear the site for the building of Wells Court flats (see page 28).

The demolition of the Crown and Sceptre public house at the corner of Crown Street and High Street, 27 July 1961. Next to the pub is Graves' butchers shop and beyond that Wilcox's tobacconist and confectioner.

A police officer taking details at the scene of an accident in Cecilia Street, 17 October 1952.

Ma Minter's shop in St Helens Street was a wonderful example of the type of small shop that sold 'everything'. Close inspection shows Hacks cough sweets, cigarettes, sweet drinks, peas, chocolates, tins of soup, and much more.

Minter's shop was part of this row which was demolished to make way for Wells Court flats.

St Helens Street, from the crossroads of Grimwade Street and Argyle Street, in the 1950s. These shops were also demolished to make way for Wells Court flats. They included (from the left) G. Deeks, estate agent and house furnisher, F.J. Ansell, radio engineer, King and Waters, opticians, S.R. Ilott, greengrocer, and Bartlett's hairdressers.

The Bond Street fire station, which used to house horse-drawn steam fire pumps, closed when the new fire station opened in Colchester Road in the mid-1960s.

These photographs show Colonel Hardy addressing the residents of Wells Street in the 1950s. He was there to inform them about the plans to redevelop the street. A table complete with cloth was set out for him in the middle of the street and the residents listened carefully to his announcement.

Wells Street, with its tiny terraced houses.

All gone – the demolition of Wells Street is complete. St Helens School is on the right.

These fine houses in Foundation Street were demolished in the mid-1960s and a multi-storey car park now stands on the site.

Wingfield Street, 29 November 1962. The Phoenix public house stands at the corner. All this area was cleared to make way for a multi-storey car park.

The demolition of houses in White Elm Street, 16 January 1959.

Great Whip Street, with Felaw Street off to the right, in the 1950s. The house on the left is the one featured in the picture on pages 30–1. The sign on the side of Haward's bakers shop on the right directs passengers to the *River Lady* (*see* page 65).

Heavy summer rain caused flooding in Ranelagh Road in June 1958. The engineering works of Reavell and Company Ltd is on the left.

Wherstead Road was flooded in another summer storm in July 1963.

Winter snow being cleared by an Ipswich Council Highways Department snow plough in the early 1960s. Egerton's garage used to dominate this part of Crown Street but its site is now occupied by Crown Pools.

Westgate Street looking towards the Cornhill, 27 January 1965. At this time traffic flowed through what is now a pedestrianized area. The businesses on the left were John Collier, tailors, Stones television and radio, the Crown and Anchor Hotel, and Footman & Pretty's general store. On the right were the Oriental Restaurant, W.H. Smith, Paige Gowns, costumiers, Smith & Sons, cleaners, and Dolcis shoe shop. The union flag was flying at half-mast as a mark of respect following the death of Sir Winston Churchill three days earlier.

Westgate Street during the 1950s. This is the reverse view to the picture shown opposite. Halfway along on the right, at the corner of Providence Street, was the 'Fifty Shilling' tailors shop. The name of this shop gives an indication as to values at the time.

The Christmas lights in Westgate Street, 1964.

Princes Street, looking towards the town centre, September 1960. All these buildings have since been demolished. Today, the roundabout linking Franciscan Way and Civic Drive is in the centre of this view. On the right is Latimer's garage and the Friars Inn on the corner of Portman Street.

The mid-1960s saw huge changes in this part of Princes Street. The Greyfriars development was under construction as the old buildings in the area were demolished, including Spurling's auctioneers and Latimer's garage.

The Corn Exchange in operation, 26 February 1957. This building was also the home of the produce market until it moved to the Greyfriars development in the mid-1960s.

Road traffic was often brought to a standstill as railway trucks were moved across the road to and from the dock area near Stoke Bridge. This steam tram engine, on shunting duties, was photographed in operation on 1 March 1952.

Queen Elizabeth II's Coronation Day, 2 June 1953, saw celebrations all over town, despite the poor weather. A carnival procession made its way through the town centre, watched by thousands of people who braved the weather to attend the celebrations. The procession is passing through Westgate Street.

The Coronation procession passes from Carr Street into Tavern Street.

An American-theme float mounted on a vehicle from one of the US bases, in Tavern Street.

A girls' brigade band marching through Tavern Street during the Coronation procession.

A Coronation party in James Street for residents from Edgar Street, Portman Street, and Priory Street. These tiny houses and streets were lost when the Greyfriars development was built in the mid-1960s (*see* page 118).

The Coronation was one of the BBC's first major outside broadcast events. Although reception in Ipswich was far from good, thousands watched the event on television; for many of them it was their first experience of this relatively new medium. These elderly residents were invited to watch the set at Holywells Mansion.

Houses being demolished in Crown Street, near the junction with High Street, 15 June 1959. Every building shown here has gone, including the William Pretty factory on the right, which was demolished in the 1980s.

Crown Street Congregational Church at the corner of High Street, September 1964. Offices now stand on this site.

The demolition of Harmony Square in the 1950s. This was off Woodbridge Road between Lacey Street and North Hill Road.

Brewers Stuart & Patterson brought a horse-drawn dray to town as a publicity exercise on 19 August 1958. Here shoppers watch as the dray passes Ridley & Son's shop in Tavern Street.

When it stopped at the Selkirk public house in Selkirk Road, this crowd, mostly children, gathered round the horses.

ACKNOWLEDGEMENTS

Many thanks to all those who have contributed to my collection of old photographs over recent years. Without their interest and help my series of books featuring Ipswich in the past would not have been possible.

Special thanks are owed to:

Colin Barber • Phil Hilton • Peter Swinger • Christine and Michael Hyde
Ralph Chinery • Derrick Neave • Cecilia Davey • Keith Locke
the late Mr and Mrs W.C.S. Girling • H.N. James